EARTH'S
NATURAL
BIOMES

FOREST

BIOMES

Louise and Richard Spilsbury

Crabtree Publishing Company
www.crabtreebooks.com

Crabtree Publishing Company
www.crabtreebooks.com
1-800-387-7650

Published in Canada
Crabtree Publishing
616 Welland Avenue
St. Catharines, ON
L2M 5V6

Published in the United States
Crabtree Publishing
PMB 59051
350 Fifth Ave, 59th Floor
New York, NY 10118

Published in 2018 by CRABTREE PUBLISHING COMPANY.

First published in 2017 by Wayland
Copyright © Wayland, 2017

Authors: Louise Spilsbury, Richard Spilsbury

Editors: Hayley Fairhead, Philip Gebhardt

Design: Smart Design Studio

Map (page 9) by Stefan Chabluk

Editorial director: Kathy Middleton

Proofreader: Lorna Notsch

Prepress technician: Tammy McGarr

Print and production coordinator: Margaret Amy Salter

Photographs

All photographs except where mentioned supplied by Nature Picture Library www.naturepl.com

Front cover(main), p5 and p32 Klein & Hubert; title page(main) and p6 David Norton; p4 Floris van Breugel; imprint page(b) and p7 Luis Quinta; title page(b) and p8 John Abbott; contents page(t) and p9 main Nick Garbutt; back cover(l), title page(t) and p10 Jussi Murtosaari; p11 Eric Baccega; back cover(r) and p12 Luiz Claudio Marigo; front cover(b), imprint page(t) and p13 Mark Bowler; p14 Chris Mattison; p15 and p31(b) Matthew Maran; p16 Pascal Pittorino; front cover(tl) and p17 Andy Rouse; p18(main) Tim Laman; p19 Doug Wechsler; p20 Bernard Castelein; front cover(tr) and p21 Alex Hyde; p22 Cyril Ruoso; p23 and p31(t) Jabruson; p24 Jabruson; p25 Pete Oxford; contents(b) and p26 Aflo; p27 Pete Oxford; p28 Suzi Eszterhas; p29 Ian Lockwood.

Photographs supplied by Shutterstock: p9(inset) Hashim Pudiyapura;

Photographs supplied by Wikimedia: p18(inset) Bcameron54.

Printed in the USA/122019/BG20171102

Library and Archives Canada Cataloguing in Publication

Spilsbury, Louise, author
    Forest biomes / Louise Spilsbury, Richard Spilsbury.

(Earth's natural biomes)
Includes index.
Issued in print and electronic formats.
ISBN 978-0-7787-3993-7 (hardcover).--
ISBN 978-0-7787-4037-7 (softcover).--
ISBN 978-1-4271-2003-8 (HTML)

    1. Forest ecology--Juvenile literature. 2. Forests and forestry--Juvenile literature. I. Spilsbury, Richard, 1963-, author II. Title.

QH541.5.F6S67 2018   j577.3   C2017-906885-7
                                            C2017-906886-5

Library of Congress Cataloging-in Publication Data

Names: Spilsbury, Louise, author. | Spilsbury, Richard, 1963- author.
Title: Forest biomes / Louise Spilsbury, Richard Spilsbury.
Description: New York, New York : Crabtree Publishing, 2018. | Series: Earth's natural biomes | Includes index.
Identifiers: LCCN 2017051155 (print) | LCCN 2017052936 (ebook) | ISBN 9781427120038 (Electronic HTML) | ISBN 9780778739937 (reinforced library binding) | ISBN 9780778740377 (pbk.)
Subjects: LCSH: Forest ecology--Juvenile literature. | Forests and forestry--Juvenile literature. | Forest conservation--Juvenile literature.
Classification: LCC QH541.5.F6 (ebook) | LCC QH541.5.F6 S677 2018 (print) | DDC 577.3--dc23
LC record available at https://lccn.loc.gov/2017051155

CONTENTS

WHAT ARE FORESTS?

Forest **biomes** are areas with large numbers of trees covering the land. Trees are the giants of the plant kingdom.

The trunk of this giant sequoia tree towers above the other trees in Kings Canyon National Park in California. A large tree can lift 100 gallons (380 liters) of water out of the ground in just one day.

Trees in all shapes and sizes

Trees grow in forests worldwide, but only in places with enough rainfall so their roots can take up enough water to survive. They range from enormous redwoods and sequoias, which are the biggest living things on Earth, down to slender birch trees. They can have tiny leaves shaped like needles, or giant, flat leaves. But, however different, they have two things in common. They all have big, tough, woody stems that support them, and they can live for many years.

Amazing Adaptation

Adaptations are special features or body parts that living things develop over time to help them survive in a biome. Trees get energy for growing so big from food. Like other green plants, they are adapted for making their own food by **photosynthesis**. Inside tree leaves, energy from sunlight is used to turn carbon dioxide gas from the air, and water supplied through its roots, into sugary food.

Forest life

Forests are not just about trees. Many living things have adapted to life in the forest biome. Plants, such as ferns and orchids, grow on the branches, and **fungi** grow on the forest floor. Some animals, such as insects and monkeys, eat tree leaves and fruit, and others, including wild boar and deer, eat fallen nuts. Many **predators**, such as jaguars and chameleons, survive by catching forest **prey**.

Vital resource

During photosynthesis, plants release oxygen. Nearly all living things on Earth need oxygen to survive, as it is used to release energy from food in a process called respiration. Two-thirds of the total leaf area of all land plants in the world is found in forests, so forests are essential oxygen factories supporting life on our planet.

Chameleons are lizards that use branch-gripping feet to move through forests. They have long tongues to catch insect prey they have spotted with their swivelling eyes.

Fact Focus: Biome or Habitat?

Biomes are regions of the world, such as deserts, forests, rivers, oceans, tundra, and grassland, that have a similar **climate**, plants, and animals. A biome may be made of several **habitats**. A habitat is the specific place in a biome where a plant or animal lives.

TYPES OF FORESTS

Forests can be divided into four main types: taiga, **deciduous**, temperate rain forest, and tropical rain forest. Each type has distinct characteristics and is composed of specific kinds of trees.

Boreal Forest

The boreal forest, or taiga, is found in the coldest parts of Earth, where there is just enough water in the soil, which is not frozen, for trees to survive. Taiga has mostly **coniferous** trees, such as pine, spruce, and fir, which make seeds in cones. These trees have leaves all year and grow close together, so little light reaches the forest floor.

Deciduous forest

Deciduous trees, including oak, beech, maple, and chestnut, have leaves that change color and fall to the ground in autumn. The trees remain bare through dark winters, surviving on stored food in their trunks. Then in spring, new leaves appear and begin to make food.

Amazing Adaptation

Many coniferous trees have needle leaves (see page 10). They have a small surface area so they do not lose much water by **evaporation**. Holding on to water is important for trees when there is limited water in the soil. Needles also have a wax layer on the surface that protects them from cold and snow.

In a deciduous forest, leaves turn yellow, red, orange, purple, and brown as they lose chlorophyll, the chemical that gives leaves their green color and carries out photosynthesis.

Rain forest

Some forests grow in places where the annual rainfall exceeds 80 inches (200 cm). This abundant moisture allows trees to grow very tall. Most of the tallest rainforest trees form a continuous **canopy**, or roof, over the forest. These plants get the most light.

Beneath the canopy, smaller trees and other plants, such as shrubs, survive using the light that filters through from above. The damp branches of trees are covered in **epiphytes**, which are plants that grow on other plants. These include mosses, orchids, and ferns. Vines reach the light by twisting upward around tree trunks.

Tropical or temperate?

There are two types of rain forest. Tropical rain forests grow in places that are hot all year round and are very humid, as water on the ground evaporates. Typical trees include figs, mahogany, kapok, and eucalyptuses. Temperate rain forests grow in cooler places and typical trees include cedars, redwoods, and cypresses.

In tropical rain forests, some tall trees, such as this fan palm, grow wide surface roots at ground level. These buttress roots act as stabilizers to support the trees' great height.

FORESTS AROUND THE WORLD

Forests cover around one-third of all land on Earth. This biome is found in many areas throughout the world. However, the polar regions and mountaintops are too cold, and desert areas are too dry and often too hot for trees to grow.

Moderate climate

Deciduous forests grow in western and central Europe, northeast Asia, and eastern North America. Here the climate is temperate, which means the temperature is not too cold and not too hot. There is rain (and sometimes snow) throughout the year. The fallen leaves break down, or **decompose**, into **nutrients** that make the soil rich. All year round, there are gaps in the canopy that let light in. Nutrients and light help many plants grow on the forest floor.

Moderate and wet

The biggest area of temperate rain forest is along the west coast of North America, where the temperate climate is made wetter by rain and mist arriving off the Pacific Ocean. Temperate rain forest is also found in damp parts of South America, Japan, New Zealand, and the United Kingdom.

Mosses grow on the trunks of these trees in a temperate rain forest in Washington State.

Northern forest

The boreal forest covers more land than other forest types. It is found in a large area stretching from North America to across northern Europe and into Russia. There are two main seasons in the boreal forest: a short, warm, and wet summer, when trees do most of their growing, and a long, cold, and dry winter. The boreal forest floor is dark and also low in nutrients, so not much grows beneath the trees.

The tropics

Most rain forests grow in tropical areas. The tropics are areas north and south of the equator. There is much rain in the tropics, and most rain forests get more than 100 inches (250 cm) of rain every year. Year-round warm temperatures average 65°F (18°C). There is never any snow or frost. With perfect growth conditions, it's no surprise that there can be 750 species of trees in a four-square-mile (10-square-km) patch.

Rain forests create their own rain, too. A lot of the rain that falls on rain forests never reaches the ground. Instead, it stays on the trees because the leaves act as a shield. In other regions, rain evaporates and is carried away to fall as rain in far–off areas, but in rain forests, 50 percent of the precipitation comes from its own evaporation.

Amazing Adaptation

Tropical rainforest leaves often have drip tips to make rain pour off quickly during downpours. As a result, fungi and **bacteria** cannot grow on the surface in the humid conditions.

This map shows where the main boreal forest, deciduous forest, tropical rain forest, and temperate rain forest areas are located around the world.

Arctic Ocean

Europe

North America

Atlantic Ocean

Asia

Africa

Pacific Ocean

Pacific Ocean

South America

Indian Ocean

Australia

■ Boreal forest
☐ Deciduous forest
☐ Tropical rain forest
☐ Temperate rain forest

Antarctica

9

BOREAL FOREST LIFE

The boreal forests are home to a wide range of animals that have different ways of dealing with the varying seasons and surviving in the biome.

Seasonal foods

In the short boreal forest summer, leaf-eating animals, from caterpillars to deer, tuck into new, tender leaves on the boreal forest trees. Insects, such as butterflies, flies, moths, and wood ants, are active, and usually have their young in this warm season.

The boreal forest becomes quieter in the harsh cold of winter. Many insects die, but their young may survive over winter, hidden under bark on trees. Some insect-eating birds, like sandpipers, move to warmer places farther south, but other birds stay put. Crossbills have a year-round food supply because they eat the oil-rich seeds in the cones of coniferous trees.

The tip of each half of a crossbill's beak crosses over the other. The bird twists the lower half away from the top half to open the scales on a cone. The crossbill sticks its tongue into the gap to pull out the seed inside.

Taiga residents

Some animals stay in the boreal forest all year long. Small plant-eating, or **herbivore**, mammals include snowshoe hares, squirrels, and voles. They survive the cold using different adaptations. For example, squirrels stay warm by sleeping in protective drays (nests).

Larger herbivores include deer and moose. Moose angle their heads back when running through dense vegetation. By doing this, the moose flattens its antlers, so they don't snag on bushes and trees, allowing the moose to run faster to escape predators.

The boreal forest herbivores face the threat of predators as well as the cold. Boreal forest predators range from wild cats and pine martens to wolves. A moose can weigh ten times as much as a wolf, but a pack of wolves can attack and kill a moose by working together.

Amazing Adaptation

Large herbivores, such as moose, lose heat more slowly than smaller animals in the cold, long winters of the boreal forest.

Moose eat leaves of broadleaved boreal forest trees, such as birch, mosses on tree branches, and grasses in forest clearings.

TROPICAL RAINFOREST LIFE

There is a remarkable richness of life in tropical rain forests. This forest biome covers just six percent of Earth's land, yet has over half of all known species of animals and plants!

Life in the trees

Many animals are perfectly adapted to live their whole lives in the canopy. For example, tree frogs have sucker-shaped feet to grip onto bark and leaves. Sloths move slowly through the branches, hanging upside down from long, curved claws, grazing on leaves. Many monkeys and apes travel through the canopy in search of food, such as fruit and leaves. Gibbons swing along from branch to branch using massively powerful arms and shoulders.

The spider monkey's tail tip can curl around and grip branches. Hanging from its tail like a rope, the monkey can concentrate on selecting and plucking the freshest leaves.

Fact File: Salonga National Park

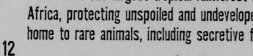

Location: Democratic Republic of Congo
Size: 13,900 sq. mi. (36,000 km²)
Overview: The largest tropical rainforest **reserve** in Africa, protecting unspoiled and undeveloped forest, and home to rare animals, including secretive forest elephants.

Insect universe

The range of types of living things in a biome is called **biodiversity**. Tropical rain forests have an enormous biodiversity of insect life. These rain forests are home to 80 percent of all known insect species on our planet! They include giants of the insect world, such as 12-inch (30-cm) stick insects, and butterflies the width of a dinner plate. There are remarkable insect predators, such as praying mantises, which have giant arms with claws, which can shoot forward to spear victims.

A trip into this forest can be uncomfortable because of the abundance of insects, including swarms of blood-sucking flies, such as mosquitoes, and irritating sweat bees that land on people to drink the sweat off their skin! On the forest floor and all over the trees there are millions of ants, such as leafcutter and army ants, in search of food. Many live and move around in giant groups or colonies.

Leafcutter ants cut out pieces of leaf with their jaws and then carry them back to the nest balanced on their heads!

Amazing Adaptation

In the dark, humid interior of a leafcutter ant nest, the **colony** has a fungi garden, which it keeps supplied with leaves. Leaves are impossible for the ants to digest, but the fungi can decompose the leaves into sugars, which are eaten by the ants.

TEMPERATE RAINFOREST LIFE

The damp, misty, cool world of temperate rain forests is dominated by trees, such as redwoods and sequoias. These can grow more than 330 feet (100 m) tall and weigh hundreds of tons.

The forest floor

The giant trees of the temperate rain forest can live for thousands of years, but when they die, they leave a big hole in the canopy. New trees and other plants, such as sorrel and laurel, can grow in the patches of sunlight on the rich soil formed from decomposing trunks and leaves. The sodden, mossy soil is home to animals, including slugs and salamanders. Salamanders wriggle on short legs through the mosses hunting worms and ants, usually at night.

Amazing Adaptation

When threatened, an Ensatina salamander stands stiff-legged on its toes, arches its back down, and flips its tail toward the attacker. This shows off the bright underside of its tail, which has many glands that release sticky, milky poison.

The Ensatina salamander, found in the western part of the United States, has brown skin on top for **camouflage** on the forest floor, and orange skin underneath to warn predators, such as snakes, about its poisonous skin.

Bears in the forest

Temperate rain forests are often home to grizzly, brown, and black bears. Black bears are the smallest of the three and are at most 6 feet (2 m) long and weigh 600 pounds (270 kg). Black bears are the most common bear found in the temperate rain forest. They use their long, tough claws for climbing and for digging into rotten trunks to unearth beetle **larvae** to eat, or to rip open bees' nests to get at the honey inside.

Black bears have a heavy coat of thick hair that not only keeps them warm in cool winters, but also dry in the damp forest air. During winter, there is less food in the forest. That's why black bears fatten up during summer when food, including shrub berries, is abundant.

Black bears can climb fast and high up trees, in search of eggs to eat, to hide from predators, such as coyotes, or to find a quiet spot to sleep.

Fact File: Fiordland National Park

Location: New Zealand
Size: 4,825 sq. mi. (12,500 km²)
Overview: The largest national park in New Zealand protects temperate rain forest of southern beech trees, along with flightless birds, including kiwi and kakapo, a type of parrot.

DECIDUOUS FOREST LIFE

Deciduous forests provide shelter and food for a wide range of animals. Some, such as bumble bees and hoverflies, feed on the **nectar** of flowers that bloom before the new leaves emerge in spring.

Tree food

Deciduous trees provide food for many animals through the seasons. Some insects, such as moth caterpillars, nibble on leaves.

Others, such as cicadas, pierce the tree to drink the **sap** flowing through tubes inside the tree. Deer scrape off and eat bark, while squirrels feed on and store nuts to last the winter. Wild boar and badgers snuffle through the **leaf litter** in search of fallen nuts, insects, fungi, and any other food they might come across.

Amazing Adaptation

Young cicadas burrow up to 9 feet (2.5 m) underground and feed on sap in tree roots. Some types remain here for up to 17 years avoiding predators, before burrowing out, climbing trees and changing into adults. Then predators with much shorter life cycles, such as wasps, will have forgotten cicadas were ever there!

Mouth

Cicadas have a short, sharp mouth shaped like a tube to pierce thick bark and wood to reach sap inside the tree.

Stripes and spots

Stripes and spots are patterns used as camouflage by different deciduous forest animals. This coloration is an adaptation for blending in with the fallen deciduous leaves, patches of dappled shade under the canopy, and even areas of tall grasses in clearings. For example, fallow deer have spots on their backs, wild boars have horizontal stripes, and tigers have vertical black stripes on orange and white. Because tigers are difficult to spot, they can get close to and pounce on unsuspecting prey. This is helped by soft pads on the tiger's large paws, which help it to walk almost silently over dry leaves on the forest floor.

Tigers live in temperate deciduous forests in India and Nepal.

Fact File: Chitwan National Park

Location: Nepal
Size: 360 sq. mi. (932 km^2)
Overview: A reserve and World Heritage Site with a wide variety of forest plants, including bamboo and deciduous sal trees. This reserve is home to Bengal tigers and the one-horned rhinoceros.

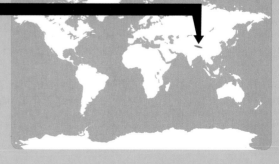

FOREST LIFE CYCLES

The forest biome is the scene for some amazing and varied life cycles. A life cycle is the journey from egg to adult animal, or seed to adult plant.

Locked up!

When a female hornbill is ready to lay eggs, she climbs into a nest space inside a hollow tree and uses mud and poop to close up the hole, leaving just a tiny slit. The mud dries hard so she is locked in! She lays her eggs and waits until the young hatch, grow, and develop feathers to fly before breaking out. She relies on her male mate to bring food for her and her young. This behavior keeps out predators, such as snakes and other hornbills, that might kill the young when they are tiny.

The female hornbill stays imprisoned inside the tree until her hatched chicks grow too big for the space. Then she breaks them out!

Amazing Adaptation

Tree frogs live in the canopy far from ponds where they could lay eggs. Some solve this problem by laying their eggs in pools of water collected in **epiphyte** plants on branches in the canopy. The tadpoles eat insects that fall in this watery habitat or other eggs their mother places there specially as food.

Ichneumon wasp

The female ichneumon wasp hovers over a tree trunk flicking her antennae. She feels vibrations from her prey: a larva munching through the wood inside. Then she injects an egg into the larva she has located. Her egg hatches into a wasp larva that eats the prey from the inside. Once fattened up over winter, the wasp larva transforms into an adult ichneumon wasp that burrows out of the wood.

The ichneumon raises her back end and bores a long, sharp tube through the wood to inject an egg into her prey hidden beneath the surface.

Brazil nut trees

Brazil nut tree seeds (brazil nuts) thud to the ground in very strong seed pods the size of grapefruits. Agoutis are rat-like mammals with big, chisel-shaped teeth tough enough to bite into the pod. They eat some nuts on the spot, but also stuff their cheeks with others and carry them off to bury elsewhere in the forest for a future snack. With luck, a forgotten nut will **germinate** and have more space and sunlight to grow than under the canopy tree it fell from.

FOREST FOOD CHAINS

When a forest animal eats a plant or another animal, some of that energy passes to the second animal. A **food chain** shows who eats whom and therefore, who receives the energy.

The links in a chain

Any living thing needs energy to survive. The primary source of energy in all biomes is sunlight. In the forest biome, it is mostly trees that convert this energy into food by photosynthesis.

The next link in the chain is the herbivores, which take in some of that energy by eating leaves, fruit, bark, roots, and nuts.

Then the animal-eaters, or **carnivores**, get in on the action by eating herbivores and other carnivores. For example, in the forests of Madagascar, lemurs eat tree leaves and fruit, and cat-like fossas eat lemurs.

Amazing Adaptation

The fossa hunts lemurs and other fast-moving prey in its forest food chain. It uses retractable claws to grip tree bark and a long tail as a **counterbalance**. Consequently, the fossa doesn't fall during high-speed chases of prey through the canopy.

Fact Focus: Food Webs

Food webs show how many living things can be connected by different food chains. For example, insects and rabbits eat plants. Frogs eat insects. Foxes eat rabbits. Snakes eat rabbits and frogs. Hawks and owls eat snakes.

Final links

The fallen leaves, branches, dead animals, animal poop, and other waste on the forest floor are an energy source for the final links in the forest food chain. These are **scavengers**, such as slugs, snails, millipedes, and worms, and **decomposers**, including fungi and bacteria. Decomposers gain energy as they feed, but also release nutrients into the soil that trees and other plants can use to grow.

Not all forest soils are rich in nutrients. Surprisingly, tropical rainforest soils are thin and low in nutrients. Dead matter, such as leaves, that falls from the trees decomposes rapidly in the humid conditions. But the tree roots grow in a mat over the soil and absorb the nutrients before they can get deep into the soil.

These extraordinary cup-shaped mushrooms are part of the fungi that have invaded and are speeding the decomposition of a fallen tree in a forest biome.

PEOPLE AND THE FOREST BIOME

Forest biomes are places where many people live. They can find most or all of the things they need to survive in the forest—from the animals they hunt for food to the materials needed for shelter.

Indigenous peoples

There are many distinct groups of **Indigenous** peoples with particular beliefs, languages, and identities living in various parts of the forest biome around the world. For example, in the Amazon tropical rain forest alone there are around one million Indigenous peoples spread across some 400 nations. Indigenous peoples living in the boreal forest include the Aleut peoples of Alaska and the Yakut peoples of Russia.

Baka nation

The Baka peoples of Central Africa are traditionally hunter-gatherers. Some hunt game, such as deer, using spears and bows and arrows, and make temporary camps in the forest as they move around. Many Baka peoples live in permanent villages. They farm crops to trade along with forest foods such as honey, and make products to sell, such as baskets from plant fibers.

A Baka mother and her child shelter in a temporary hut made from sticks and ngongo leaves in a tropical rain forest in Cameroon, Central Africa.

Changing population

Human populations in forests are constantly changing. Foresters, farmers, and miners are some of the people who travel each year to the forest biome to live and work. Settlements grow as more newcomers need places to live, shop, and trade.

Forest tourism

Some tourists visit forests to get close to remarkable biodiversity in a natural habitat, rather than in zoos or wildlife parks. For example, in some rain forests there are high-wire walkways that lead visitors into the canopy. Other tourists hike or mountain bike along forest trails.

Not all forest communities have proper roads. This makes it hard for workers and tourists to travel around the forest, and to move forest products, without getting stuck in the mud.

FOREST RESOURCES

For centuries, forests have provided important resources that people need and want, such as wood and water.

Wood

The most obvious tree resource is wood, which can be used to make a variety of timber products. Hardwoods, such as sapele or beech, are cut into planks to make furniture and sometimes musical instruments. The planks can also be sliced and glued together to make plywood used for construction. Wood from coniferous trees, called softwoods, is also widely used to make buildings and also ground into wood pulp to make paper.

Fact Focus: Fuelwood

Globally, around 2.5 billion people, or over a third of Earth's total population, rely on **fuelwood**. It is often foraged from forest and burned to cook food. Some people also use charcoal, a black fuel made by heating and drying wood.

This African hardwood tree has been cut down by loggers with powerful chainsaws to be used for timber.

Non-timber resources

Forest plants provide many resources beyond timber. These include fruit, nuts, bark, and leaves, which can be used as foods, raw materials, or even ingredients in a broad range of medicines. Rainforest flowers are the basis for some important cancer treatments.

Forests also conceal resources. The land under some forests is a store of valuable and useful **minerals**. For example, beneath the boreal forest are reserves of coal, oil, iron, silver, gold, and diamonds.

This forester in Guyana, South America, is cutting into a tree's bark to allow latex to ooze out and collect in a container. The latex is used to make natural rubber.

Water supplies

Forests create and clean water supplies. The soil, along with leaf litter, soaks up rainwater in the forest floor. The soil cleans the water by absorbing all the pollutants and gradually releases the clean water into streams, rivers, and **groundwater** supplies. A forest can also prevent flooding on land by storing water in its soil after heavy downpours.

FOREST THREATS

Deforestation is the biggest threat to forests, and it is increasing as the global population grows. Up to 58,000 square miles (150,000 square km) of forest is lost every year—the equivalent of losing 48 NFL football fields every minute.

Out of control

Logging companies cut and remove whole trees from forests. The cutting is controlled in some places, but it often happens illegally, even in protected forests, because of the demand for rare and valuable hardwoods. People also clear forests by burning in order to farm or mine. Fires can rapidly get out of control, especially if **peat** soil catches fire.

Fact Focus: Global Warming

Global warming is the rise in Earth's average temperature. This is caused by heat being trapped in the atmosphere by **greenhouse gases**, such as carbon dioxide.

Deforestation makes global warming worse. With fewer trees, there is less photosynthesis and less carbon dioxide being removed from the atmosphere. As well, burning waste wood produces more carbon dioxide.

A rain forest in Brazil burns in order to clear the land for farming. Forest fires present an immense danger to forest life and humans, not only from spreading fire, but also from choking smoke.

Major impacts

Deforestation has major impacts on forest life. Animals are killed directly in forest fires and by loggers. Roads, settlements, and farmland can break up areas of forest into smaller, isolated patches. In such **fragmented** habitats, animals may not be able to find enough food or meet other animals to breed. Roads allow better access into the remaining forest not only for legal activities, but also for illegal hunting and logging.

Foresters sometimes create plantations on cleared land, but these new forests have few tree species and are treated with chemicals, so they cannot support biodiversity like natural forests. Farmland where tropical rain forest once stood often cannot grow crops for long, because the soil is low in nutrients. Consequently, farmers abandon this land and cut down more forest.

This soldier in Central Africa has confiscated illegally hunted forest deer, called duiker. This prevents the hunters from making money by selling the meat.

Fact Focus: Natural Threats

Natural deforestation can occur after natural disasters, such as volcanic eruptions and forest fires started by lightning strikes. It can also occur when insects invade and kill trees. For example, emerald ash borer beetles kill ash trees by feeding under the bark, which stops the flow of water and sap.

FOREST FUTURES

Forests are an astonishing and critically important biome for all inhabitants of our planet. This is the reason why people are working to protect them now and for the future.

This baby orangutan's mother was killed by loggers. In this forest reserve in Borneo, Indonesia, caregivers took care of it as an infant. Now they are helping it to explore the biome and find food so it can look after itself in the rain forest.

Reserves

Only around ten percent of global forests are protected, which is about half the area of the United States. Governments and charities fence off areas of forest and employ **rangers** to watch out for hunters and illegal logging. Usually, there are too few rangers for a large area, so people use satellites to help spot illegal activities. Most conservation efforts are directed at forests with high conservation value because they have unusual or well-known species, such as orangutans, or rich biodiversity.

Fact File: Olympic Forest Reserve

Location: Brazil
Size: 0.4 sq. miles (1 square km)
Overview: This reserve protects a small section of the biodiverse Atlantic Forest in Brazil. It was funded by a public appeal for donations during the Olympic Games in Rio in 2016. The reserve protects endangered animals, including woolly spider monkeys and crowned eagles.

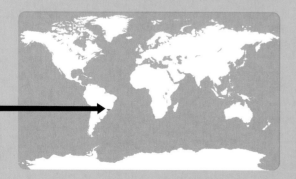

Changing habits

People are protecting forests by making sure they buy wood or timber products only from legally logged forests that are **sustainable**. Sustainable forestry means logging some trees, but not the oldest and rarest sorts, and replanting with young trees of similar species to retain forest cover and biodiversity. Others are establishing new forests by planting new trees.

In many forests, scientists are working to study forest life to better understand the impacts of deforestation, as well as the future impacts of global warming on forests. Their knowledge and advice can help us change our habits to protect this planet's forest future.

Time to reestablish lost forest! These women in Bangladesh are helping to plant rubber trees to create a new forest area.

GLOSSARY

adaptation Special feature or behavior that helps a living thing survive

bacteria Tiny living things that can cause diseases or decompose waste

biodiversity Variety of life or range of living things in an area

biome Large region of Earth with living things adapted to the typical climate, soils, and other features

camouflage Color, pattern, or shape that makes it hard to identify an object against its background

canopy Main leafy layer of a forest

carnivore Meat-eating animal

climate Typical weather pattern through the year in an area

colony Group of individuals living together

coniferous Tree that makes seeds in cones

counterbalance Weight balancing another weight

deciduous Trees with leaves that fall as a response to a drop in temperature

decompose Break down into simpler pieces

decomposer Living things that break down dead plants, animals, and waste

deforestation Destruction and removal of forest

epiphyte Plant that grows on another, larger plant

evaporation Change of state from liquid to gas

food chain A way of showing the movement of the sun's energy from one living thing to another

food web A network of related food chains that show how energy is passed from one living thing to another

fragmented Broken up into smaller, unconnected pieces

fuelwood Wood used primarily to burn for cooking or warming homes

fungi Living things, such as mushrooms, that feed on dead plant and animal matter

germinate When a young plant emerges from a seed

global warming Rise in average temperature of Earth caused by human activity

greenhouse gas Gas, such as carbon dioxide, that traps the sun's heat in the atmosphere

groundwater Water under the ground that supplies springs and wells

habitat Place where an animal or plant typically lives

herbivore Plant-eating animal

Indigenous Peoples who have lived in a place for a very long time, and have strong historical and cultural associations with the land

larva Young stage of insects and other animals

leaf litter Part of forest soil made from decomposing dead leaves releasing nutrients

logging Cutting down and removing trees

mineral A substance such as salt that is nonliving and forms naturally, usually in the ground

nectar Sweet liquid made in flowers

nutrient Chemical substances essential for living things to be healthy, grow, and live

peat Soil made from partly decomposed plants, which is often in a bog

photosynthesis Process by which green plants make sugary food using sunlight

predator Animal that hunts and eats other animals

prey Animals hunted and eaten by others

ranger Person who helps to protect a place

reserve Area protected to keep living things and landscapes of special interest safe from people

sap Fluid transported inside a plant

scavenger Animal that feeds on dead animals, plants, or waste

sustainable Able to be maintained without damaging natural resources

FIND OUT MORE

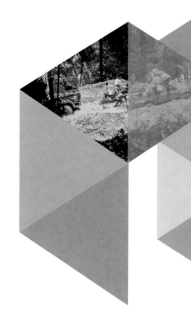

Books

Amazon Rainforest Research Journal
Natalie Hyde
Crabtree Publishing, 2018

Forests Inside Out
James Bow
Crabtree Publishing, 2015

Ultimate Explorer Field Guide: Trees
Patricia Daniels
National Geographic Kids, 2017

Websites

Check out more facts about the biome at:
www.ucmp.berkeley.edu/exhibits/biomes/forests.php

Compare the contrasting world biomes at:
http://kids.nceas.ucsb.edu/biomes/index.html

Discover all you need to know about tropical rain forests at:
http://kids.mongabay.com/

Learn amazing facts about the Amazon rain forest here:
www.natgeokids.com/za/discover/geography/physical-geography/amazon-facts/

Check out this site for live webcam footage of forest wildlife:
www.worldlandtrust.org/webcams/ornithos1

INDEX